OVERCOMING STOCKHOLM SYNDROME

*How to Break Free from Toxic Relationships
and Thrive After Trauma Bonding*

KENNETH C. HAYS

TABLE OF CONTENTS

CHAPTER 1. INTRODUCTION

Evelyn was stuck in a bad relationship. Her partner, Alex, was sometimes nice but often got really mad. Every time she tried to leave, Alex said sorry and promised to be better, so she stayed.

Her friends warned her about Alex, but she thought she could help him. She felt like it was her job to fix him because he seemed so troubled. She thought nobody understood what she was going through.

As time went by, she started feeling worse about herself because Alex kept controlling her. She always defended him, even when people said bad things about him. She didn't realize how bad things had gotten.

Then, one day, she had a moment of clarity. She realized that being with Alex was making her feel awful. She decided she had to leave.

It was really hard. Alex begged her to stay and said he would change, but she knew she deserved better. With help from a therapist and her friends, she finally broke free from Alex's hold. She escaped from the bad relationship and found herself again. It wasn't easy, and she had to try many times, but she did it. She was finally free from the bad feelings and could look forward to a happier future.

Stockholm Syndrome was first observed in 1973 when a failed bank robbery led to a six-day hostage situation in Stockholm, Sweden. In this situation, the bank robber was caught but the hostages were defending him. They claimed they feared for their lives and believed that the kidnappers' kindness was proof that they weren't going to kill them. While this was the first time that this term was used, this phenomenon was not new. Many people have found themselves in similar situations (emotionally and/or physically dangerous situations) and formed a bond with the very person who has put them in that situation.

In these cases, it has been common for the victim to have sentiments of mistrust or anger that is not in line with the experience and may at times be a direct contrast to how they feel about that person. Over time, these strong feelings become internalized as a bond with the abuser. This bond is unbreakable and explains why victims sometimes fight on behalf of the abuser. This is because the bond is a survival strategy for the victim. He/she must side with the abuser to survive. Feelings of helplessness and perceived lack of support/misunderstanding from others ("No one understands what I am going through!") can cause the victim to feel he/she is the only person who can understand or help the abuser and that it is their responsibility to do so.

The reasons for this are clear. If the abuser is a significant other, the hope is that the abuser will change and the situation will improve, so the victim is seeking to comfort the abuser and stop provoking their anger. If the abuser is a parent, the victim may feel that it is he/she who should be taking care of the parent. This bond and the reasons for forming it comprise the essence of trauma bonding and are key to understanding this concept.

1.1 DEFINITION OF STOCKHOLM SYNDROME

Stockholm syndrome is a psychological state of mind that occurs when a person experiences an extraordinary situation that has stirred up various emotional responses. The most common characteristics of Stockholm syndrome fall into three basic categories:

(1) the sense of being in danger and the conviction that one's captor is prepared to act on that threat;

(2) the captive's impression of the captor's modest acts of compassion in the midst of a terrifying situation; and

(3) isolation from viewpoints other than the captor's.

In short, Stockholm syndrome is the bonding between the hostage and the captor where the captive develops loyalty to the captor despite the dangerous, life-threatening, or otherwise unfavorable situation. This "loyalty" can be merely a survival mechanism, it does not have to be a conscious decision, and the effects can be long-lasting. Unfortunately, Stockholm syndrome is a very common occurrence in abusive relationships and it is very detrimental to the victim of the abuse.

1.2 UNDERSTANDING TOXIC RELATIONSHIPS

Toxic relationships involve patterns of behavior where the victim finds themselves in a position of validating a consistently destructive identity. They're driven by the hope that they can change the other person and get their needs met, at the expense of their own identity and emotional well-being. This is often because the person is also toxic, and any form of self-improvement or attempt to enforce a healthy boundary will be seen as a threat and will be met with opposition. The toxic person is still a person, and more often than not, they're coming from a place of pain. They may not necessarily be bad people, but it's not a healthy or constructive relationship if they're anchored in their pain and there's nothing you can do to guide them out of it. In some cases, a toxic person could actually be a great influence on you or someone you know because they've changed and it's always

possible to change, but that's not the person you're dealing with, and unfortunately, change has to come from within. This highlights the negative impact and also further emphasizes the fact that it was never their intention to become a toxic relationship.

1.3 Impact of Trauma Bonding

Stockholm Syndrome has often been cited as a cause of trauma bonding. However, trauma bonding doesn't just impact hostages but many victims of domestic abuse. Bonding with the abuser can cause conflict in the victim's mind between what is right and wrong, and a sense of allegiance to the abuser, even with knowledge of the abuser's wrongdoing. Bonding can cause the victim to overlook the abuser's faults and lead them to believe they can change the abuser. Victims of severe abuse may adopt learned helplessness and begin to believe that they

deserve the abuser and the treatment that they receive. Withdrawal from the trauma bond can have psychological and physical symptoms including depression, cognitive dissonance, emotional imbalance, and in severe cases, the onset of post-traumatic stress disorder if the bond is broken by force such as police intervention or the death of the abuser.

Trauma bonding has been described as the misuse of fear, excitement, and sexual feelings to bond the victim to the abuser. Everyone who has been a victim of abuse has likely experienced some form of trauma bonding. High amounts of both good and negative emotions are created by abusers in order to strengthen their link with their victim. This bond is powerful and makes it hard for the victim to release the relationship, no matter how much he or she knows it is in his or her best interest. This is why some victims of abuse have been known to mourn the loss of the relationship and abuser,

even if they know the relationship was killing them.

Chapter's Summary

- ❖ Understand the three basic categories that contribute to Stockholm syndrome: the sense of danger, perceived acts of compassion from the captor, and isolation from alternative viewpoints.

- ❖ Toxic relationships involve patterns of behavior where the victim validates a destructive identity, hoping to change the other person at the expense of their own well-being.

- ❖ Trauma bonding, often associated with Stockholm Syndrome, can occur in abusive relationships, leading victims to overlook the abuser's faults and believe they can change them, causing psychological and physical symptoms when attempting to break the bond.

CHAPTER 2. RECOGNIZING THE SIGNS

Abuse is the improper usage or treatment of something, often to unfairly or improperly gain benefit. Abuse can come in many forms and can be both physical and non-physical. It manifests as a pattern of behavior that a person uses to gain and maintain power and control over another. Forms of non-physical abuse come in two main categories: covert abuse and overt abuse. Covert abuse is hidden or undercover and it can take many forms. It is ambiguous and often does not feel like abuse, making it hard to understand or identify. Overt abuse is open and obvious and can often be defined and addressed. Abuse can have lasting impacts on a person's quality of life. An adult intimate relationship is a way of establishing control for the abusive person, where the person being abused loses control. This manifests as a power imbalance. The power imbalance is the core dynamic of abuse and the abuser feels entirely justified in using any tactic which helps to maintain and/or increase the power. Abuse is not occasional and is a pattern of behavior that often gets more severe with time. It is uncommon for an abusive person to change without outside intervention. Abuse may occur more often after a breakup or when the victim begins to exhibit independent behavior.

Manipulative behaviors are those that are used to get what a person wants, ignoring what the other person wants or needs. Manipulative behaviors can be identified by their intent to get the other person to do what the manipulator wants. They can be learned and used for a purpose. Manipulative people often have poor communication skills and try to be indirect to avoid rejection. They also tend to be self-centered, and using manipulative behaviors helps them meet their goals with little concern for the other person's feelings. In identifying manipulative behaviors, it is important to look at the intent of the behavior. A behavior may be well intended but come across poorly, or it may be intentional and hurtful. Once intent is established, it is easier to figure out the best way to address the problematic behavior. It's also important to look at context. Sometimes a behavior that looks manipulative has a reasonable explanation.

2.1 IDENTIFYING MANIPULATIVE BEHAVIORS

Manipulative behavior involves the three classic components of intentional behavior that are designed to control another person, with the use of tactics such as bribery, withholding, distortion, and sabotage. From the perspective of the one being manipulated, the result is often a 'crazy-making' sense of cognitive dissonance as the manipulator tries to have them believe the false and self-serving version of reality that the manipulator is presenting, and an internal battle between self-doubt and a 'gut' feeling that something is wrong. However, with the reality distortion and reinforcement of behaviors being so powerful and frequent, the person can be left doubting their perceptions and experiences. This can be cemented by defining one's reality of the current experience of life and the world as inherently replete with deep-seated personal defects, weaknesses, and damaged fabric of identity. This often pushes people to feel that they are incapable of making their own decisions and setting the direction for their lives. This demoralization into a sense of learned helplessness is a key feature of depression and can pose a major barrier to seeking recovery from abusive relationships.

2.2 EMOTIONAL AND PSYCHOLOGICAL ABUSE

Emotional abuse is often so covert that

recognizing it can be difficult. It's frequently minimized and sometimes it's even dismissed because there are no bruises. Many people even think that it is not abuse. There are no immediately visible marks, making it even harder to prove the abuse. This doesn't mean that it is in any way less damaging for the victim. It can cause more long-term trauma than physical abuse. Often one form of abuse will bleed into another and in many cases, several forms of abuse listed here will occur simultaneously. Toxic relationships erode the victim's sense of self; the victim becomes disoriented and is unable to experience the clarity of their perceptions. Often the abuser will invalidate the victim's feelings with the intent of having the victim think they are wrong or 'crazy'. This serves the abuser in making the victim think the abuse is their fault. Invalidation of the victim's feelings belittles the victim; invalidation of perceptions induces a sense of disorientation and disables the victim from being able to tell the difference between right and wrong. Often the abuser will intentionally confuse the victim and present a false image in the victim's mind to cause the victim to be more pliable and easier to control. Hostility is a clear sign of abuse, and an emotionally abusive person displays this consistently whether or not in an argument. There are three forms of hostility: overt, thinly veiled, and covert. Overt hostility is openly aggressive behavior, thinly veiled hostility is negative or critical behavior disguised in a pleasant tone, and covert hostility is when the abuser behaves in a way to makes the victim feel hurt or neglected.

2.3 ISOLATION AND CONTROL TACTICS

This can be one of the most damaging tactics that a captor can use because as of recently it has been more recognized as being a form of abuse. The act of isolating someone from their friends and family takes away a person's support system and increases their reliance on the abuser. It is very dangerous because it occurs in small steps. It can be something as simple as getting angry when the victim spends time with their friends rather than them, and escalate to extreme measures, like moving to a different state. This tactic is a very effective way of causing the victim to feel completely dependent on the captor, for socialization is a very important part of human life, and taking that away will cause great discomfort. The rare occasion of socialization with people who are supportive and caring can have huge effects on a victim's morale and self-esteem. The captor will frequently associate the time spent with those people as the cause for any amount of trouble in their relationship with the victim, leading to obvious consequences for the victim. Captors may try to turn friends and family against the victim for added control and a way to further destroy the support system. In addition to isolation, monitoring, and control of the victims' actions outside of the home is common. Often the captor will try to control what the victim does with the day, through monetary control or other methods. In some cases, there are threats to keep the victim from seeking employment or attaining higher education. In a study conducted at California State University, it was found that victims of same-sex domestic violence reported employment sabotage at a rate of 28%, which is a significantly higher percentage than opposite-sex cases (McClennen 382). An abuser will also use control methods to monitor when the victim goes out without them and where they are going. All of it contributes to the feeling of having no free will and no control over one's life, which is an objective of the captor.

2.4 Gaslighting and Denial

One of the more insidious forms of emotional and psychological abuse is referred to as gaslighting. This behavior is used to cause the victim to doubt their memory, perception, and sanity. The phrase originated from a play where a husband tries to make his wife insane by turning down the gas lights in their house. When the wife notices the change in light, the husband denies that there is any change. This is the key point of gaslighting, to attempt to convince the victim that they are imagining things, that their memory is incorrect, and to destabilize their grasp on what is truly happening. This often leaves the victim feeling confused and with a lowered self-esteem. It's important to note that anyone is capable of gaslighting, and it is not limited to the abuser or abusers' personality. Oftentimes, it is a learned behavior from one's family of origin. Coming from a place where there was mental illness, denial, and/or a lack of accountability have proportionately higher incidences of gaslighting behavior. Situation stress or crisis can also bring out the behavior in an individual who has not previously shown it. A very chronic form of gaslighting can easily lead the victim to be diagnosed with depression, or in some cases, it can mimic the behavior of someone with depression, causing the victim to believe that they are indeed mentally ill.

Chapter's Summary

- ❖ Understand that abuse can be both physical and non-physical, including covert and overt forms.
- ❖ Learn to recognize manipulative behaviors such as bribery, withholding, distortion, and sabotage, which are used to control others.

❖ Emotional abuse can be covert and difficult to recognize, often eroding the victim's sense of self and causing long-term trauma.

❖ Isolating victims from support networks and controlling their actions are common tactics used to maintain power and dependency.

❖ Gaslighting is a manipulative tactic aimed at making the victim doubt their memory and perception, leading to confusion and lowered self-esteem.

CHAPTER 3. WHY YOU MIGHT BOND WITH YOUR ABUSER

Imagine being trapped in a bad relationship. You're constantly criticized, belittled, or even threatened. It might feel crazy, but here's the thing: you might start to care about the person hurting you. That's Stockholm Syndrome in a nutshell. Let's break down why this happens.

3.1 PSYCHOLOGICAL MECHANISMS AT PLAY

Being in an abusive relationship is like being held hostage. You're constantly on edge, never knowing what might set your partner off. Your brain kicks into survival mode. If your partner throws you a crumb of kindness, like not yelling for a day, it feels like a win. You cling to that feeling, hoping for more. This creates a messed-up sense of gratitude towards someone who's hurting you.

Another trick your brain plays is emotional

detachment. You might downplay the abuse, convincing yourself it's not that bad. It's a way to cope with the constant fear and stress. It's like putting on a mental shield to protect yourself.

3.2 THE ROLE OF SURVIVAL INSTINCTS

Humans are wired to survive. When threatened, we cooperate. In an abusive relationship, you might act submissive or even defend your partner's actions, hoping to avoid getting hurt. It's like trying to appease a bully. You might even start to see your partner as a protector, which is completely messed up, but it's your brain's way of trying to keep you safe.

3.3 TRAUMA BONDING

The longer you're in an abusive relationship, the stronger the trauma bond becomes. It's like an intense connection built on shared experiences, even if those experiences are awful. Your partner might be the only person you see regularly, becoming your only source of comfort, even if that comfort comes with a price. This creates a warped sense of loyalty and affection for the very person hurting you.

3.4 COGNITIVE DISSONANCE

Imagine believing something and then doing the opposite. That's cognitive dissonance, and it's uncomfortable. It will conflict with your need for safety and happiness if you begin to take care of your abuser. To ease this discomfort, you might convince yourself the abuse isn't that bad, or even blame yourself. It's your brain's way of trying to make sense of a crazy situation.

Remember: It's Not Your Fault. You deserve to be safe and happy. The next chapter will explore ways to break free from this unhealthy bond.

Chapter's Summary

- ❖ Be aware of moments of kindness from an abuser, as they can create a false sense of loyalty and gratitude.
- ❖ Don't downplay or minimize abuse to cope; acknowledge the harm and seek support.
- ❖ Don't defend or justify abusive behavior; prioritize your safety and well-being.
- ❖ Build supportive relationships outside of the abusive one to break the cycle of trauma bonding.
- ❖ Confront conflicting beliefs and actions to regain control and break free from the abusive relationship.

CHAPTER 4. BREAKING FREE

During the early stages of the trauma bond, leaving the relationship is the last thing a you would consider. But breaking the cycle of abuse is an important factor for recovery. After an abusive relationship, it is possible to have a happy and healthy life with the correct resources and assistance. Many victims of abuse, particularly those who have Battered Woman Syndrome, may not survive long after leaving an abusive relationship. It is important to create a safety plan before deciding to leave the relationship. This includes deciding where to go in an emergency, i.e. a friend's or relative's house, or a local domestic violence shelter, having a suitcase packed and hidden, and having important documents copied and stored in a safe place. It is crucial that once the decision has been made to leave, you must not, under any circumstances, let your abuser know you are planning to leave.

4.1 BUILDING A SUPPORT SYSTEM

The support of caring and understanding people is an integral part of recovery from Stockholm Syndrome. Your support system can provide you with reality checks, a means of escaping your situation by providing places to stay and other aid, and by helping you to learn to trust again. Since one of the symptoms produced after Stockholm Syndrome generally can involve ongoing, repetitious, or disturbing thoughts about the abusive situation and mixed or confused emotions, support from friends, family, and group members can help reduce the possible feelings of alienation, isolation, and depression. It is often true that family members and friends of victims have been hurt by the changes in the victim. They blame themselves for not "stopping it" sooner and this guilt can change the way they interact with the victim. The group educates family and friends of victims and survivors to provide a comprehensive understanding of Stockholm Syndrome. We welcome and encourage family and friends to join the group and communicate with other members. This will help them understand the changes that have occurred and promote needed discussions to aid in the recovery process for both parties.

4.2 SEEKING PROFESSIONAL HELP

Legal advice can be an essential part of breaking free from an abusive relationship. A family lawyer will be able to provide information on your legal rights and options. You may require a lawyer to represent you in proceedings regarding separation, children, property, and finances. If you have been the victim of a crime, such as assault or stalking, you may choose to seek compensation through a criminal injuries compensation scheme. Information on these schemes will generally be available from your support agency or a legal practitioner. Since legal matters can be complex, it is helpful to obtain advice from a lawyer who specializes in family law or a community legal center that can provide information and assistance at a lower cost.

Professional assistance provides an opportunity to explore your feelings and find healthier patterns of thinking and behaving. This can lead to an overall improvement in the quality of your life. If your relationship has significantly impaired your capacity to function, you may require the support of a mental health professional. Therapy can be very empowering as it provides an opportunity to focus on yourself in a way that you may have been unable to do in the past. It often involves setting goals and learning strategies for both immediate and long-term changes. This might involve making some difficult decisions. A therapist can help you examine your options in a safe and objective setting. Therapy need not be long-term, but it can be an investment in your future self. A psychiatrist is a medical doctor who has done extra training to specialize in psychiatry. This means they can diagnose mental and physical problems, prescribe medication, and admit people to the hospital. If you are having difficulty with mood, thinking, or behavior, it may be worth seeking their opinion.

4.3 ESTABLISHING BOUNDARIES AND SELF-CARE

Self-care involves being in tune with your feelings and responses and taking active steps to preserve your physical and mental well-being. Often people in abusive situations become disconnected from themselves and are forced to neglect their own needs. Self-care involves re-learning to nurture and care for yourself, in the same respectful and compassionate way that you would do for a friend. This can involve something as simple as allowing yourself to rest when you are tired, or permitting yourself to do something that you find enjoyable. An important aspect of self-care is also recognizing and distancing yourself from activities and people that are harmful to you. This is why practicing good boundary setting is a crucial aspect of self -care.

In attempting to establish a life free from abuse and exploitation, it is essential to identify and practice ways of taking care of oneself. This involves recognizing that you are a worthwhile person and that you deserve to be treated well. Establishing boundaries is vital in achieving this. It involves recognizing the need to limit the rights of others to act in ways that are harmful to you. It also involves being aware of your rights and of your responsibility to protect yourself from being exploited or abused. Boundaries can be set in terms of physical limits, privacy, and personal information, and in terms of how you allow yourself to be treated by others. Liaising with a good friend or therapist can help develop your boundary-setting skills.

4.4 DEVELOPING EMPOWERMENT STRATEGIES

Once you begin the process of reaching out for support, seeking information, or redrawing your boundaries, you are likely to encounter further challenges from the abusive individual. It is important to prepare for these, as they are likely to undermine your progress. You might want to consider recapping your reasons for leaving and the reality of the abuse, rehearsing what you will say to any manipulation, and enlisting further support from friends or a support group. It is often a relief to stop focusing on the abuser and put the energy back into focusing on yourself. What are your hopes and dreams? What have you always wanted to do but were prevented by the abuser or your inner fear? Begin doing more of these things, and anything which makes you feel good about yourself. You might consider setting yourself some small goals or challenges. This could be as simple as starting a new book, trying out a new recipe, or taking up a new hobby. Now that you are taking some of the focus of survival and addressing your state of mind, it's well worth considering seeking emotional support. This is somewhere else to put some of your energy: into understanding more about how to read relationships, identifying your emotions, and healing from your past. This may feel overwhelming at times but remember, the journey of a thousand miles starts with a single step! This is also a good time to start addressing any addictions (to substances, food, self-harm, etc.) that could have developed during the abuse, as this is another way of taking the focus back to yourself and addressing your state of mind.

Chapter's Summary

- ❖ Develop a safety plan before leaving an abusive relationship to ensure protection and secrecy from the abuser.
- ❖ Build a support system of caring individuals to provide emotional assistance, reality checks, and practical aid.
- ❖ Consult legal and mental health professionals for legal rights, therapy, and empowerment strategies.
- ❖ Establish boundaries, practice self-care, and recognize your worth to foster emotional and physical well-being.

❖ Prepare for challenges from the abuser, focus on personal goals and dreams, and seek emotional support to reclaim control and build a fulfilling life.

CHAPTER 5. HEALING AND RECOVERY

Deep and persistent feelings of betrayal, shame, and worthlessness often make you struggling with the effects of trauma from the relationship and continuing to feel victimized long after the relationship has ended. Getting past these feelings involves accepting that the trauma occurred and developing healthy ways to cope with the memories when they occur. It also involves addressing any grief caused by the loss of the relationship, idealization of the relationship, or by the realization of the truth of the relationship. Seeking closure by taking the time to understand and mourn the true nature of the relationship and the hopes one had invested in the relationship often helps make the final break from the relationship and move on. Therapy is an immensely helpful tool in understanding and addressing trauma and grief. Cognitive-behavioral therapy and dialectical behavior therapy can be particularly helpful in understanding the connection between thoughts, feelings, and behaviors in developing healthy coping strategies and building mastery over trauma reminders. Rebuilding self-esteem and self-worth is integral to the overall task of rebuilding one's life and moving on after a toxic relationship. It involves being compassionate and understanding of yourself, accepting that the abuse was not your fault and that the abuser alone is responsible for the abuse and its effects. A helpful exercise is to write a list of the great things about yourself and keep it as a reminder that you are a worthwhile and good person. Goal setting and goal achievement can also be very effective in building self-efficacy. Scheduling and engaging in pleasurable and mastery activities provides further mastery experiences and enhances the belief that one can competently cope with adversity in the future. In severe cases of abuse where post-traumatic stress and its effects are overwhelming, professional help may be necessary to address these issues and rebuild self-esteem and self-worth.

5.1 Processing Trauma and Grief

Grief is another emotional hurdle that must be overcome. Accepting the truth about the abusive relationship could lead to the loss of the person who provided safety and security, no matter how false this was. In many cases, you will have to relocate, change jobs, and even change identity to ensure safety from your abuser. This can all represent major loss and change, which can be difficult to cope with. Grieving the actual losses, as well as the loss of what could have been, a happy and healthy relationship with the abuser, has to happen so that you can come to the last stage of grieving, which is acceptance. Acceptance of what allows for true closure and the ability to move on.

Trauma is defined as a deeply distressing or disturbing experience. This can mean different things for different people, but for victims of Stockholm Syndrome-defined abusive relationships, this means years of manipulation, control, and in many cases, physical and emotional abuse. It can take years to accept the reality of what you have been through and to begin processing the feelings that come along with it. As a victim, you must work through anger, guilt, and depression and eventually come to some level of acceptance. Support groups and therapy can be very helpful in this process, as well as finding a creative and constructive outlet for all the emotions that will undoubtedly arise.

5.2 REBUILDING SELF-ESTEEM AND SELF-WORTH

People who have been emotionally or physically abused at some point in their lives are the most likely to have low self-worth. They best know the self-doubt and self-loathing that come from being abused. The first thing to understand about self-worth is that it is a belief. It is something that we decide to believe about ourselves, it is not a truth. If you were in an abusive relationship, you are likely an expert in self-blame. It is important to remember that it does not matter what happened in the relationship, whether or not at times you think you didn't help things or even provoked your partner, you never deserved the abuse. People with healthy self-worth who have never been abused will also have provoked people in their lives at times, it is part of being human. The difference is that one person was able to forgive themselves. Abusers decide to abuse, it is their responsibility and theirs alone. You are not responsible for the abuse. You can base your new foundation for self-worth on the fact that you've survived a terrible relationship, but now you're taking the steps to heal and move on. This takes an enormous amount of strength and courage. Tell yourself how brave you are for moving forward. This is the truth. This is also self-affirmation. Self-affirmations are positive statements that focus on a certain quality that we would like to build on. An example might be "I accept and love myself unconditionally". This may be hard to say at first as it is hard to believe, but that's the point, it's something to build on. A technique that can be used to dissolve negative beliefs and emotions many have found helpful is EFT (emotional freedom technique), also known as tapping. EFT is based on the Chinese meridian theory and is a way of balancing one's energy system. This alone may sound ridiculous, but for those who have tried it, the results can be astonishing. If one's self-worth is very low, it is best to consult a therapist who is experienced with abuse issues and who can provide advice specific to the individual's case. This is also true for a lot of the following information. A therapist has the skills to help one rebuild their self-worth. While a support group can help greatly by seeing that others have or are going through the same thing, and while friends can provide love and encouragement, sometimes people need something more, something that can provide more insight and that deals specifically with the issues at hand.

5.3 RECONNECTING WITH PERSONAL IDENTITY

When we are in a toxic or abusive relationship for a long time, we tend to lose sight of who we are, often becoming an extension of our abuser and losing our interests, opinions, and even our identity. This occurs due to a co-opting of the victim's identity and life by the abuser to have a living reflection of themselves and to increase dependency on the victim. This makes it very difficult when leaving the relationship to know who we are, what we enjoy, and even how to function. We can only travel as far on the road of life as our level of self-identity will allow. Without knowing who we are, it's impossible to know what we want from life and we become easy prey to being involved in future toxic relationships. A strong sense of self-identity will enable us to have conviction in our likes and dislikes, enabling us to make clear and decisive decisions about what we want in our lives. This will enable us to attract healthy relationships and repel the unhealthy ones, promoting our emotional and psychological safety. Being a strong and confident person with a well-defined self-identity acts as an immune system to future abuse. A person who knows who they are and what they want from life is a hard target for an abuser. Eroding your sense of self and replacing it with your abuser's identity is what keeps the you in the relationship and makes it hard for you to leave.

5.4 CULTIVATING HEALTHY RELATIONSHIPS

To begin to cultivate healthy relationships, you first need to identify what a healthy relationship consists of. Identifying what your values and rights are is an important step in determining what is healthy and what is not. A healthy relationship will be based on mutual respect, trust, equality, honesty, support, and good communication. In a healthy relationship, decisions are made together and compromises are made. There is an understanding that both parties have the right to their own opinions and the right to make their own decisions for themselves. With your identified rights and values from previous steps, develop a list of what is healthy for you in relationships and what is unhealthy. This provides a guide to what you will and will not accept in relationships and will help to keep you on track with developing healthy relationships in the future. Changing the types of people you associate with is important in cultivating healthy relationships. In the past, you may have been drawn to people who presented the same qualities as your abuser. It is important to realize that not everyone is the same and that there are many good people out there. You may want to discuss your ideas of what is healthy and unhealthy with a trusted friend or family member for another opinion. At first, you may find healthy people boring or unattractive because they are unfamiliar. This is a sign that you need to persevere and stay on course with developing relationships with these people. As you become more self-assured and comfortable with your list of what is healthy and unhealthy, you will find it easier to recognize positive and negative qualities in others. Building and keeping good relationships requires skills. Unfortunately, these are skills that you may not have had the opportunity to develop. Good communication skills are an important factor. This involves not only expressing yourself but also active listening. This means giving the speaker your full attention, letting the speaker know you have understood them, and not becoming defensive. Problem-solving and conflict resolution are other important skills. This involves resolving disputes fairly and rationally. These skills will be easier to develop with the right people, but some awareness and effort will be required on your part.

Chapter's Summary

- ❖ Acknowledge and cope with feelings of betrayal, shame, and worthlessness from past trauma by seeking closure and therapy.

❖ Work through grief and trauma, accepting the reality of abusive relationships and mourning the losses to achieve true closure and move forward.

❖ Rebuild self-esteem by understanding the abuse was not your fault, engaging in self-affirmations, and seeking therapy or support groups.

❖ Rediscover your personal identity after leaving a toxic relationship to regain independence and attract healthy relationships.

❖ Identify and uphold values and rights in relationships, develop good communication and conflict resolution skills, and surround yourself with supportive individuals.

CHAPTER 6. THRIVING AFTER TRAUMA BONDING

Rediscovering personal goals and dreams represents the very essence of ourselves. Especially during traumatic periods of our lives where we are often actively discouraged from investing in our own futures, it is common to lose sight of what truly makes us happy and gives us fulfillment. Victims of Stockholm syndrome too often forget the person they once were and what their original aspirations in life were. It is important to revisit these ideas in a safe and positive environment. The realization of such goals, regardless of the sneers and discouragement from the abuser, can greatly assist in self-esteem building. Successes, whether large or small, can also help break the cycle of self-blame and helplessness that is manifested by the learned helplessness aspect of Stockholm Syndrome. Setting goals and taking steps to reach them, no matter how small helps to counter the dependency and dread that the victim feels because it brings a sense of control and personal efficacy to one's life. Any goal must be based on personal desire, not on the suggestion of others, for this is one of the only ways to rediscover oneself and gain freedom from the influences of the abuser.

6.1 REDISCOVERING PERSONAL GOALS AND DREAMS

Many abuse survivors report a loss of self-identity and a tendency to get lost in previous relationships or the roles they played in those relationships. In some cases, the survivor has been out of touch with whom or what they want to be and what they value for so long that this becomes a primary focus. The survivor may feel frustration at not accomplishing what they feel they are capable of and what may have been a primary goal derailed by the relationship. Some report not pursuing dreams and goals because the abuser made it seem that they were not capable of it, could not be trusted to accomplish it, or that the abuser was more deserving of that particular goal. These thoughts are part of the negative messages that were left behind and need to be cleared. To understand what you really value, enjoy, and want out of life, it is suggested that you take some quiet time alone to reflect on your life and complete a personal inventory. The following exercises are designed to uncover long-lost dreams and goals and find a new sense of direction in life.

6.2 DEVELOPING RESILIENCE AND INNER STRENGTH

There are two types of resilience: dispositional or the ability to bounce back after traumatic events and also learned or the ability to grow positively from stress. Dispositional resilience is possessed by many trauma survivors, whose ability to simply survive is commendable. The development of learned resilience is of particular importance to those seeking recovery from trauma bonding. This will involve a gradual change in thinking and behaviors; a process studied by Kohut which can be understood by comparing the individual to a tree. A tree that is bent as it grows will always grow in that direction unless very deliberate action is taken to bend it back. By recognizing that the tree is bent and that deliberate actions must be taken to change the tree's direction, the survivor is in the process of developing learned resilience. This process is facilitated through increased self-awareness and self-knowledge, helping the survivor to understand how their behavior has been affected by past experiences. By increasing awareness and understanding of the past, the survivor can actively change the future.

Recognizing that resilience and inner strength

are the foundations of recovery from trauma bonding is paramount to this process. Resilience has been defined as the process of adapting well in the face of adversity, trauma, tragedy, threats, or even significant sources of threat (Mancini & Bonanno, 2006). The identification of resilient individuals only serves to highlight the importance of resilience in the face of hardship.

6.3 Embracing Positive Change and Growth

Positive change and growth are often initially reactive steps taken in response to an emancipatory event, and it is through the facilitation of such processes that long-term change takes place for survivors of domestic violence. Reconstruction of self is essential to the development of autonomy, empowerment, and self-determination. Rediscovering who you are and who you want to be is a difficult process for many survivors like you. Your self-identities have been severely compromised through both the conditioning process and the negative events you have come to see as defining your life during the abusive relationship. You may have lost touch with aspirations and beliefs which once formed a positive self-identity. Your personal goals have often been sidelined, and self-limiting beliefs about capability can prevent you from taking steps toward change. Encouraging yourself to try new things, even if you feel you may not succeed, is important in rediscovering the extent of your capabilities. A supportive environment in which you can explore your sense of self and be free from judgment is important in assisting this process. It is often through the realization that you are not what your abuser has led you to believe you are, that you feel compelled to make changes in your life. Survivors of domestic violence have often previously attempted to make changes in their lives, only to find that it results in an increased risk of violence as the abuser seeks to maintain the status quo and prevent change to the power balance in the relationship. As such, you can be anxious about embarking on change and feel a sense of learned helplessness about your future situation. Acknowledging the difficulties and fears, it is important to encourage small steps towards the changes you want to make and to celebrate each achievement. This will provide a counter-conditioning experience, as by making changes you will begin to challenge your previously learned helplessness and will increase self-belief in your ability to shape the course of your life.

6.4 FINDING PURPOSE AND MEANING IN LIFE

In abusive relationships, so much energy is spent trying to maintain some semblance of peace and sanity within the relationship that personal goals and dreams are often forgotten, suppressed, or sacrificed. When the relationship eventually ends and you are faced with the task of rebuilding your life, you may feel ambivalent, apathetic, or even hostile towards the idea of setting goals and working towards your own definition of success. You may struggle with a sense of hopelessness about the future, believing that you are unworthy or incapable of creating a better life for yourself. You may find it helpful to begin the process of rediscovering your personal goals and dreams by writing about the things you have always wanted to do but felt unable to actually pursue. By writing about your goals, you can begin to visualize the possibility of creating a different life for yourself. This provides motivation for setting and working towards concrete goals, first on paper and then in reality. With each successive step towards a personally meaningful goal, you can gradually restore your faith in your own competence and decision-making ability. This can be an important foundation for the rebuilding of self-esteem and a sense of control over your life.

<u>Chapter's Summary</u>

- ❖ Take time to reflect on your personal goals and dreams, even amidst trauma, to reclaim your sense of self and happiness.

- ❖ Recognize your inner strength and ability to grow positively from stress, understanding that resilience is key to overcoming trauma bonding.

- ❖ Be open to positive change and growth, even if it feels daunting, as it is essential for rebuilding your life and sense of identity.

❖ Celebrate each achievement, no matter how small, to challenge learned helplessness and increase belief in your ability to shape your future.

❖ Reconnect with your personal goals and dreams, visualizing a new life for yourself and restoring faith in your competence and decision-making ability.

BONUS

AN AUDIO VERSION OF THIS BOOK.

You can listen to it anytime and anywhere you want. Simply scan this code below and the audiobook will be yours.